THE ALL NEW STYLE OF MAGAZINE-BOOKS

SDM

www.SDMLIVE.com

MP

MOCY PUBLISHING
WWW.MOCYPUBLISHING.COM

Printed by CreateSpace, An Amazon.com Company

All New Season
March 30th

Empire
WEDNESDAYS
ON **FOX**

SDM

EDITOR-IN-CHIEF
D. "Casino" Bailey
casino@sdmlive.com

EDITORAL DIRECTOR
Sheree Cranford
sheree@sdmlive.com

GRAPHIC/WEB DESIGNER
D. "Casino" Bailey
casino@sdmlive.com

A&R MANAGER
Aye Money
ayemoney@sdmlive.com

ACCOUNT EXECUTIVE
Frank Harvest Jr.
frank@sdmlive.com

PHOTOGRAPHERS
Treagen Colston
D. "Casino" Bailey

CONTRIBUTORS
April Smiley
Courtney Benjamin

COPY ORDERS & ADVERTISING OFFICE
Send Money Order or Check to:
Mocy Publishing
P.O. Box 35195
Detroit, Michigan 48235
(586) 646-8505
advertise@sdmlive.com

Copy Order Item #:
SDM Magazine Issue #5 2016
S&H Plus Retail Price - $9.99 per copy

WWW.SDMLIVE.COM

Printed by CreateSpace, An Amazon.com Company

MP
MOCY PUBLISHING

Copyright © 2016 Support Detroit Movement,
a division of Aye Money Promotions & Publishing, LLC and
Mocy Music Publishing, LLC. All rights reserved.
Printed in the U.S.A.

REAL MUSIC. REAL ENTERTAINMENT.

SD

ISSUE 5

Victoria Monet
CHICAGO RAPPER SPEAKS ON DREAMS VS. REALITY

MARK HUNTER

DETROIT PLAYWRIGHT MARK HUNTER IS COMING FROM THE STREETS TO THE STAGE

ALSO
HOLLY MONRAHH
SHAHIDAH
QUEEN BREYON
MONTE SS
JOHNYCE
+MORE

9 770317 847001

MARCH 2016 No.5
WWW.SDMLIVE.COM

CONTENTS

1

Samsung - Galaxy S7 edge 32GB - Silver or Gold Platinum Titanium (with 2-year contract) $299.99
www.bestbuy.com

2

Dell - Inspiron 2-in-1 15.6" 4K Ultra HD Touch-Screen Laptop - Intel Core i7 - 8GB Memory - 1TB Hard Drive $779.99
www.dell.com

3

Insignia™ - 48" Class (47.6" Diag.) - LED - 1080p - Smart - HDTV Roku TV $349.99
www.bestbuy.com

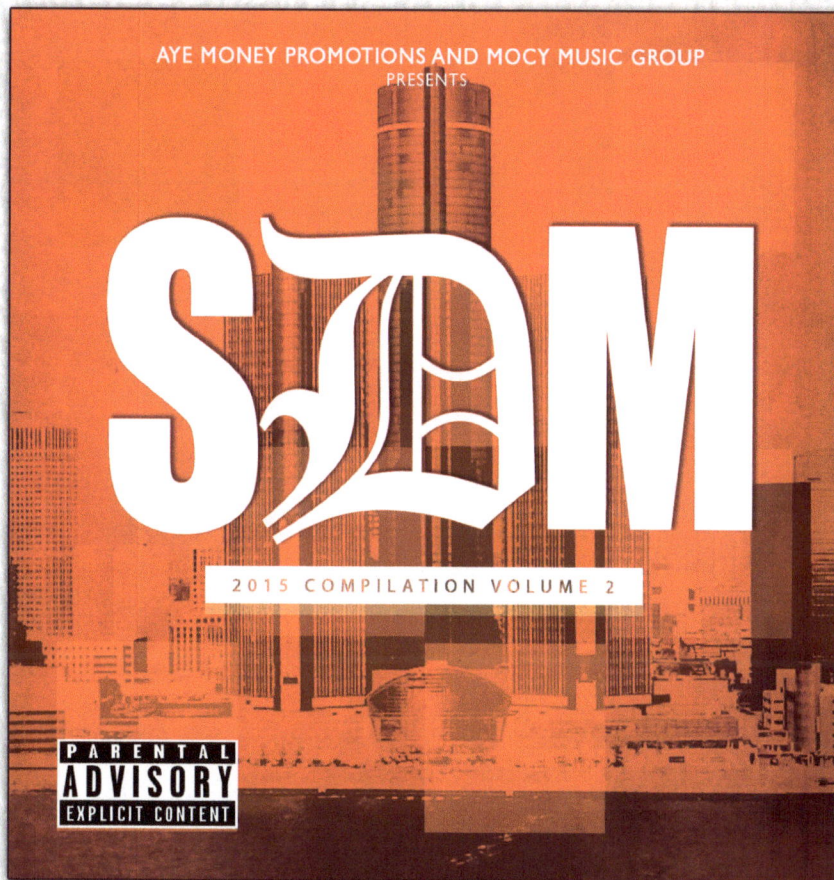

I Am Anti-Beyonce

ANTI-BEYONCE HATERS ORGANIZE A RALLY BECAUSE THEY DON'T WANT TO
SEE BEYONCE FANS GET INTO FORMATION.

by Cheraee C.

On February, 16, 2016 there was an anti-Beyonce rally held in New York, New York at the NFL Headquarters. This protest will go down in history books as the worst protest ever. What was supposed to be a rally with a bunch of angry citizens waving hateful signs and yelling stop Beyonce remarks, turned out to be a mini concert with fans from the Beyhive. A selected class of people are against Beyonce's new world tour because they disagreed with Beyonce's half-time performance at the 2016 Super Bowl 50 as it represented her blackness to the fullest extent. Beyonce's performance was associated to represent being a Blank Panther, the Black Lives Matter campaign, and paying homage to the late great Michael Jackson. A number of anti-Beyonce protesters are also trying to say that Beyonce is promoting violence against police. The Miami Police Department is another sector of people enraged by Beyonce's NFL performance and has put together a boycott against her not wanting to secure her upcoming world tour. It's not like Beyonce can't buy her own security team anyway from officers all over the world. People must've forgot that Beyonce is the unstoppable Queen Bey.

Beyonce

Happiness is a choice

#JustSoYouKnow

True To The Game The Movie

TERI WOODS IS A SELF-PUBLISHED NOVELIST WHO REVIVES ALL THE TRUTHS TO THE GAME IN HER UPCOMING MOVIE

by Cheraee C.

Authors these days are flipping their urban tales into movie scripts and hitting the big screen. The latest author to soon hit the theatre is Teri Woods. Teri Woods released her best selling novel True To The Game (book 1) which is apart of a trilogy released in 1999. Now 17 years later Teri Woods is going to bring her book to reality.

Word is the couple Quadir and Gena will be starred by Erica Peeples and Columbus Short. You may also see roles played by Draya Michelle, Vivica A. Fox, and Nelsan Ellis.

True To The Game, the novel has reportedly sold over two million copies which is why filmmakers wanted more.

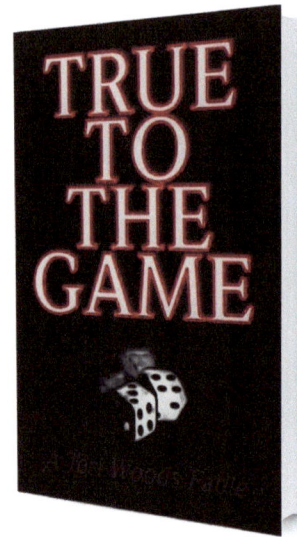

True To The Game
By Teri Woods

Available from Amazon.com and other online stores

The Black Madonna of Detroit

DETROIT'S "INDEFINABLE" HOLLY MONRAHH JUST RELEASED HER LATEST
AND GREATEST SINGLE "PI ∏" AND CONTINUES BRANDING HERSELF.

by Cheraee C.

Q. How long have you been in the music industry and how would you define yourself as an artist?

A. I have been in the music industry professionally for six years. As an artist I would define myself as indefinable. I say indefinable because every time you think you know what I'm up too, I come with a surprise.

Q. Being a woman in the industry, how do you feel like it's important to market yourself?

A. As a woman I believe we need to redefine ourselves. Having a new perception on what we see as class, beauty, sex etc. I am a woman obviously lol, I feel for all women. It all starts with your heart and mind; that determines your action so I market myself with love. That's it I stand strong, passionate, and if people don't understand love, I have to show them.

Q. When you have the right plugs and drive, your career can takeoff so how do you feel about your music career so far?

A. My music right now is fun. I've always been ahead of my time. I'm working and it feels good. I've come so far so soon and it's deeper than rap; lol my sound is changing, my soul is glowing, everything around me is changing and you will hear.

Q. How do you feel about collaborating with other artists and what artists have you worked with so far?

A. I honestly love when artists collaborate and I don't mind collaborating with artists it just has to be right. One of my early moments in my career I was a feature on Say It Ain't Tone song "What You Doing Buddy" on one of his early mixtapes as an ad lip track. Lol it was a learning experience. I've collaborated with many great artists including Rashad Morgan, Rev City, and Queen Pin just to name a few.

Q. Currently, what are you cooking up in the studio?

A. I'm in the studio right now writing for different artists as well as myself. I just dropped a video titled PI. I am so empowered to leave a mark on Earth so the music reflects legendary. I have a mixtape coming out, but I am still indecisive on exactly what to name it.

Shahidah is a Rising Star

A TALENTED SINGER AND SONGWRITER ON A MISSION TO TAKEOVER THE STREETS WITH HER VERSATILE MUSIC.

by Cheraee C.

Q. How long have you been in the music industry and how do you define yourself as an artist?

A. *Practically all my life. I started playing the trumpet when I was nine years old and the rest is history! I grew up listening to all kinds of music, oldies but goodies, pop, hip hop, R&B, alternative, country, neo-soul, etc. As a result, I try to think outside the box as it pertains to making music and I'm not afraid to take risks! I like to cover a wide range of topics. Everything from love, to heartbreak, turn-up (club) music, and everything in between! I don't limit myself to one particular style.*

Q. What experiences from your personal life have you incorporated into your music?

A. *All of my music is reflective of my personal life. On my album titled "Up Next" I talk about my experiences with love, heartbreak, haters, etc. The album is a true reflection of who I am as a person.*

Q. Describe how you managed to open up for Ryan Leslie, Teairra Marie, Juelz Santana, and Charlie Baltimore?

A. *I linked up with a promoter out in New York when I opened up for Teairra Marie, Juelz Santana, and Ryan Leslie on different occasions. I opened up for Charlie Baltimore here in Detroit at the Sunset Strip Gentleman's Club. Each we're unique, awesome experiences!*

Q. You have plenty acting avenues and artist avenues, but which avenues do you think will land you the most success and why?

A. *Hmmm… that's a tough question. I have a passion for both music and acting, but at the moment I am taking full advantage of the opportunities that are coming my way in terms of acting. As long as the doors keep opening, I'm going to keep walking through!*

Q. *I hear you did a feature with JP One so what was your experience like working with him?*

A. *I have known JP One for years. He is a good friend and colleague in the music business. He is always professional and very dedicated to his craft. We recently collaborated on his project with Nep Jennings titled "Real Motown Music" so be on the lookout for that! He was also featured in my music video "So Hood." He is a man of his word… true business man!*

Q. What is a typical day in Shahidah's life like?

A. *Every day is a constant grind! I'm a college student also so when I get home from school I am either promoting and planning for an upcoming gig (music) or rehearsing lines for a script (acting). I stay pretty busy! Once I finish an acting project, I typically have another concert/performance in the works and I start preparing myself for that. Yeah, it can get pretty hectic at times, but it's all worth it! I love what I do!*

REAL MUSIC. REAL ENTERTAINMENT.

S.D.M

ISSUE 3

KOSTA
JUST HIT THE JACKPOT WITH A NEW SMASH HIT SINGLE "LOTTERY"

BIGG DAWG BLAST
LAUNCHES THE STREET HITTA DJ'S MOVEMENT

Neisha Neshae

BRINGING IN 2016 ON STAGE WITH THE KING OF R&B R-KELLY & DROPPING A NEW MIXTAPE

PLUS MORE

THE RED CARPET EDITION
SUPERSTARS CAME WITH FASHION AT THE SDM MAGAZINE RELEASE PARTY

US - $9.99 CANADA - $14.99

01 >

9 770317 847001

JANUARY 2016 No.3
WWW.SDMLIVE.COM

Chi-Town's Finest is Victorious

VICTORIA MONET SPEAKS ON HER FAME, MUSIC, AND HER VLOG DREAMS VS. REALITY TRACKING UPCOMING ARTISTS IN HOUSTON.

by Cheraee C.

Q. Who is Victoria Monet and how did you become as famous as you are today?

A. I'm a business owner, music artist, and I was born in Dallas and raised in Chicago. I don't really consider myself "famous." I think its slight recognition, but the people that do know me now, know me because of my work ethic. I do everything I can and in my power to make things happen as far as what I want in life.

Q. Who gave you your first shot? Was it a record label, a demo, a DJ, a radio station etc?

A. It was a record label in Houston called "Grind Daily Music Group." It was me, Superstarr, Jane James (the producer), Quinn, and a few others with the label. It was my first chance to really travel and perform, record in the studio, and see how the music industry works.

Q. What is your perspective of the music industry thus far?

A. It's tough for female artists especially because there's no respect. I think guys in the industry automatically think if you're a female artist and show a little skin that means you'll give it up and to anybody, and when you don't they no longer want to work with you or continue doing business. You have to have tough skin and just know if this is what you want to do and is called to do. Do it with 1000% of you, pray about it, and God will bring the right people in your life to help.

Q. Detroit is not far from Chicago, have you entered to the D yet during your artistry?

A. I've been working hands on with Bandkamp. It's a production label out of Chicago. Shout out to Bangabeatz #Bandkamp/Def Jam. Me and him been working on artist development and getting tracks together for my next project DVD Ep "RapPorn."

Q. What is Victoria Monet currently working on?

A. I'm releasing my DVD Mixtape "The Remix Queen" soon. It's all about timing and marketing correctly. I don't want to be an average artist dropping mixtapes and no one barely knows me. We planning for this drop and then I have my "Dreams vs. Reality" Vlog on Youtube. It's my version of Love and Hip Hop, but for Houston featuring me and other artists that work just as hard and that I feel are just as talented.

Q. What made you start the Dreams vs. Reality on Youtube?

A. I've been filming behind the scenes of me being in the industry since 2009, but I decided January 2016 after I started seeing I was getting more recognition in 2014-2015 that I was going to have my own show revealing what real artists go through and have to do to make it in the industry. I've always studied other artists and loved watching those come up videos so I figured why not do my own and feature other artists on the same wave.

Q. What artists have you worked thus far?

A. My recent project has been a solo project. I've strayed from collaborations to keep from devaluing myself before I determine my worth as an artist.

Q. Where do you get your inspiration from to do music?

A. I get my inspiration from other female moguls like Rihanna, Nicki Minaj, and Tyra Banks. These are all business women that have more than one thing going for themselves and I can relate. The only difference between me and them is that they have the fame and God hasn't released my millions yet.

T.I. Joins Roc Nation

THE TRIPLE THREAT T.I., J. COLE, AND HOV NOW ON THE SAME TEAM.

by Semaja Turner

It seems as though more mainstream artists are venturing away from major record labels. Record labels don't give artists the freedoms that they want, and once you get the fame, a certain level of industry knowledge, a chain of businesses, and the billions, the world is pretty much yours.

It wasn't too long ago the King of the South T.I. left Columbia Records to be an independent artist, and just recently signed a distribution deal with Roc Nation for his 10th studio album *Dime Trap* and became the latest co-founder of Tidal making him the 19th owner in the company. For those who don't know Roc Nation is founded and owned by Jay-Z, and many artists are signed under Roc Nation including Fabolous, Big Sean, J. Cole, Kanye West, and many more.

If this decision wasn't precise or perfect timing then I don't know what is. T.I is always at the top of his music game and has been officially welcomed to the Roc Nation family.

From The Streets To The Stage

MARK HUNTER TALKS ABOUT HIS LATEST PROJECT "LET IT BURN" AND ALSO ABOUT HIS DEBUT NOVEL SET TO RELEASE THIS SUMMER.
by Cheraee C.

Q. Since your last interview with SDM, what has Michigan's favorite playwright been up to?
A. Just staying busy…being in the magazine helped me a lot. It put a light on me and the things that I'm doing so thanks. I'm just working hard and trying to make Mark Hunter and Remarkable Productions both household names. I'm getting ready to release my first novel "Daddy's Despair" and looking forward to many other projects.

Q. Can you give us a snippet of what your novel "Daddy's Despair," is about?
A. The book is really about a man willing to do any and everything to rescue his daughter from the streets. He is an ex drug dealer who changed his life once he had to get custody of his daughter, but when his daughter's life is in danger, he's willing to do whatever it takes to save her.

Q. So do you already have a publisher in mind or is the publishing part undecided and when's the anticipated release date?
A. I plan to go with Mocy Publishing LLC, and I plan to release my book sometime in June 2016.

Q. It's almost time for your stage play "Let It Burn," so will you take this play on a tour, DVD, etc and when do you plan to release your next play?
A. We're looking at dates now and I'm doing a live DVD taping in another city later this year and I plan to release my next play in October.

Q. Tell us about "Let It Burn," what is it mainly about and how did you come about finding your cast?
A. "Let It Burn" is about people dealing with situations that they need to let go of. It deals with a bad mother/daughter relationship as well as a bad marriage.

Q. You've been doing a lot of promo for "Let It Burn," so do you think that this is going to be your best play yet?

A. I think it's my best work thus far because I've learned a lot and have matured as a man and as a writer. It takes a lot to make a name for yourself in the business. A lot comes along with it and me maturing in this business has had a lot to do with the trials and tribulations that I've endured. I feel that I'm at a turning point in my career.

Q. Tell us about your team and how they have helped you make your vision come true?
A. God has blessed me with a great team of people. My director Shawnta McDougie has been able to bring my vision to life just as I had intended. You can be the best quarterback in the world, but if you don't have anyone to throw it to you won't win a game. I'm glad I finally have my team! "I'm just a man that God gave a second chance and I'm taking full advantage of it!"

Q. Tell us why you rock with Support Detroit Magazine?
A. SDM gives Detroit talent a place where they can be seen and heard.

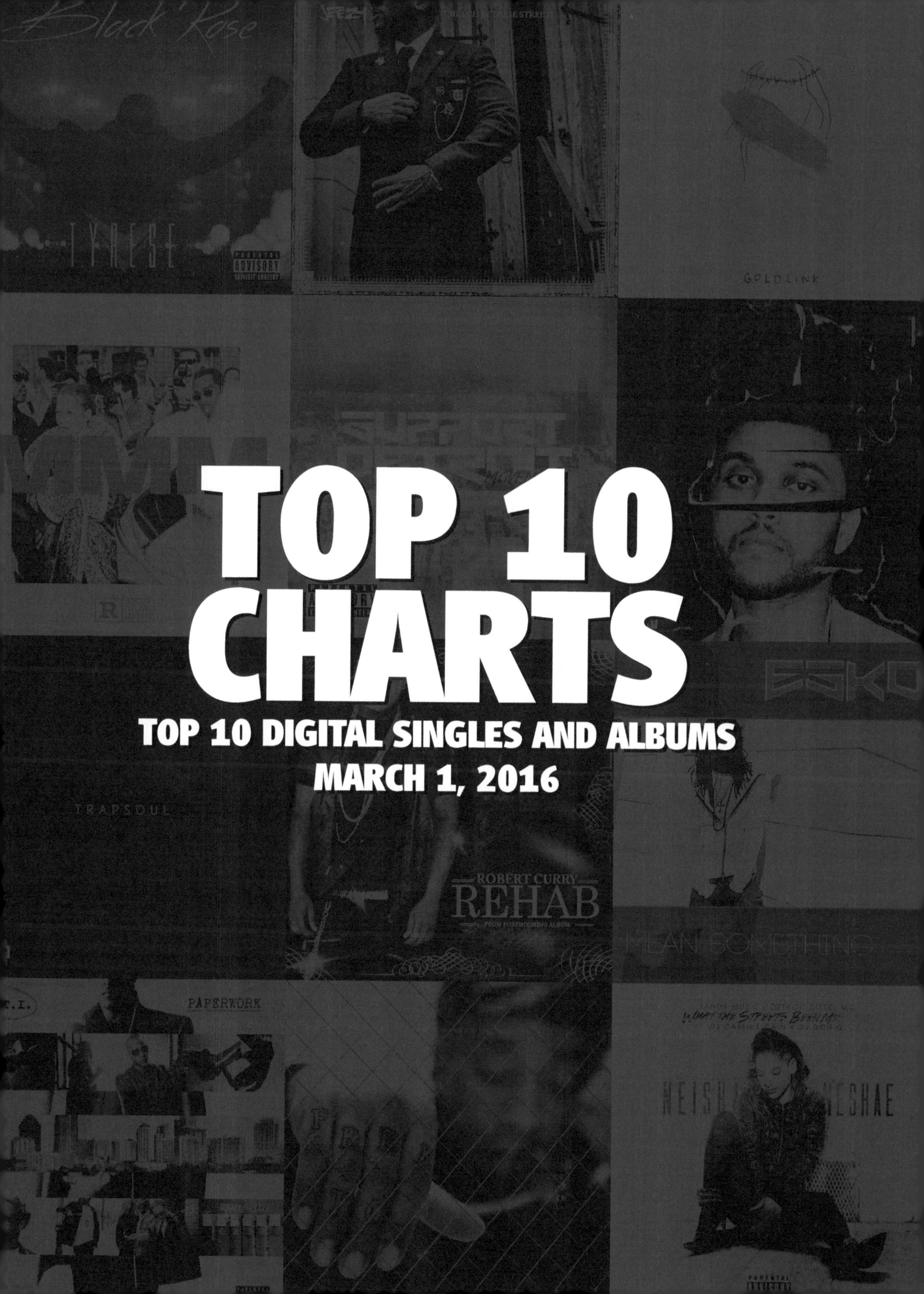

TOP 10 CHARTS

TOP 10 DIGITAL SINGLES AND ALBUMS
MARCH 1, 2016

TOP 10 CHARTS

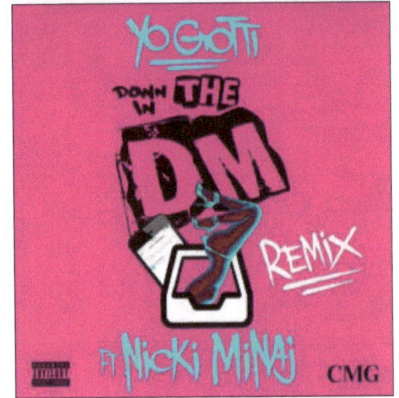

YO GOTTI ON THE VIDEO SET OF HIS HIT NEW SINGLE "DOWN IN THE DM".

TOP 10 SINGLES
CHART OF THE MONTH

No.	Artist - Song Title
1	YO GOTTI - DOWN IN THE DM FT. NICKI MINAJ
2	TYRESE - SHAME
3	JEREMIH - OUI
4	J COLE - NO ROLE MODELZ
5	KANYE WEST - REAL FRIENDS
6	NEISHA NESHAE - ON A CLOUD
7	YUNG THUG - BEST FRIEND
8	DRAKE - SUMMER SIXTEEN
9	LYNN CARTER - TOO LITTLE
10	CHRIS BROWN - LIQUOR

TOP 10 ALBUMS
CHART OF THE MONTH

No.	Artist - Album Title
1	YO GOTTI - THE ART OF HUSTLE
2	BRYSON TILLER - TRAPSOUL
3	FUTURE - EVOL
4	RIHANNA - ANTI
5	DRAKE & FUTURE - WHAT A TIME TO BE ALIVE
6	KEVIN GATES - ISLAH
7	TYRESE - BLACK ROSE
8	TANK - SEX, LOVE & PAIN II
9	J. COLE - 2014 FOREST HILLS DRIVE
10	AYE MONEY - SDM COMPILATION (VOLUME 2)

ALBUM REVIEW

TRAPSOUL

ARTIST: Bryson Tiller
REVIEWER: Cheraee C.
RATING: 4

Overnight success Bryson Tiller rising from Louisville, KY releases his latest mixtape with the radio banger "Exchange," "Talk to Me" which is Bryson's cover to Jodeci's hit "Come and Talk to Me" "How About Now freestyle" is a cover to Jordin Sparks single "How About Now", "Self-Righteous," "Two Hearts," "True Story," featuring Drake and a couple of other singles. I give his miixtape four stars.

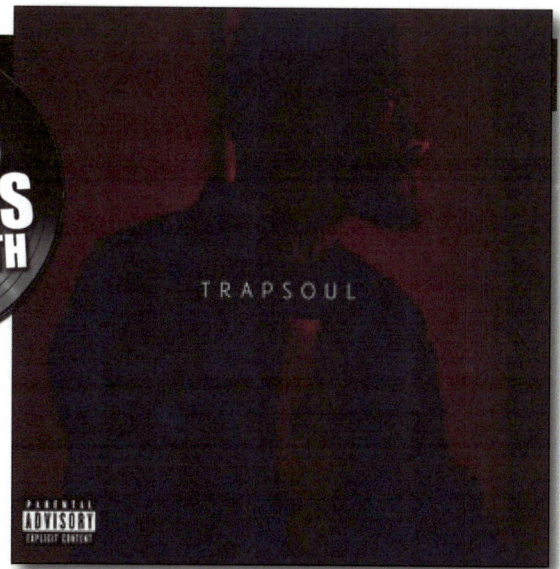

TOP 3 ALBUMS THIS MONTH

TRAPSOUL

PARENTAL ADVISORY EXPLICIT CONTENT

BLACK LIVES MATTER
www.BlackLivesMatter.com

RATE METER: 1 - WACK   2 - NEEDS WORK   3 - STRAIGHT   4 - BANGER   5 - CLASSIC

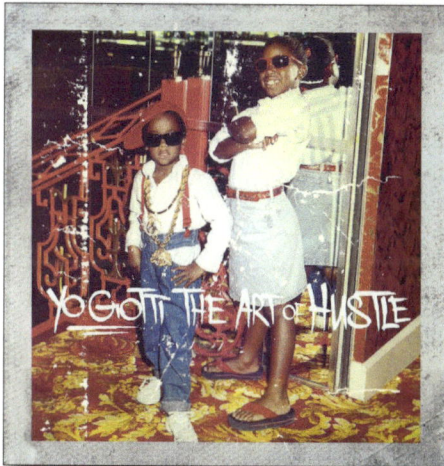

The Art of Hustle

ARTIST: Yo Gotti
REVIEWER: Cheraee C.
RATING: 4

The King of Memphis is back with another album strictly for the hustlers as he brings his fans back to the old Gotti and teaches them the laws and rules of hustling. The album includes his worldwide anthem "Down in the DM," "My City" featuring K. Michelle and features from Lil Wayne, Pusha T, Future and etc. I give the album four stars.

Evol

ARTIST: Future
REVIEWER: Cheraee C.
RATING: 4

Future has been releasing a chain of mixtapes and now his latest mixtape is titled Evol which is love spelled backwards. The mixtape includes the dope song "Low Life" featuring The Weekend, "Fly Shit Only," "Seven Rings," "Lie to Me." and some other classic singles with that one and only Future sound. I give the mixtape four stars.

HEELS & SKILLZ

Mimi Bad Azz

is am a full-time model
from Detroit, MI.

instagram
@mimi_baddazz

Photography by
@barearmy

HEELS & SKILLZ

Maybach Dukes
is a beautiful model
from Detroit, MI.

instagram
@_maybachdukes

Photography by
@barearmy

HEELS &
SKILLZ

Gabby Sky
is a sexy model
for barearmy and
lives in Miami, FL.

instagram
@missgabbysky

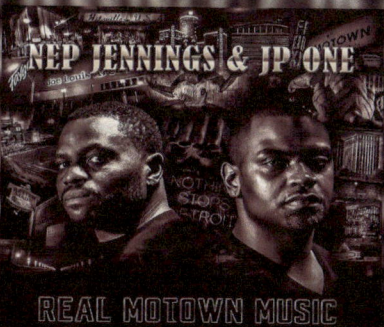
Debates Heating Up

REPUBLICAN DONALD TRUMP MAYBE WINNING WITH REPUBLICANS BUT HE IS PISSING OFF DEMOCRATS.

by Semaja Turner

Donald Trump is raising a lot of eyebrows with his political campaign to become the next president of the United States. Instead of taking an intellectual approach to gain votes, it seems like Trump has only been making a mockery of his opponents. Donald Trump supporters' have also been in the headlines for hostile behavior. In one state, a protestor from the Democrat party was punched in the face by one of Trump's supporters. There was also an episode where a young, black girl was kicked out of one of Trump's rallies by force. On the video footage, you can clearly see the young lady was walking away from the rally, but was pushed by force out the crowd. What type of politician is Donald Trump to even condone his supporters' to have such discriminatory behavior?

Although, Donald Trump has ran a campaign with comical debates, the United States election is not his Celebrity Apprentice. As of to date, Donald Trump is leading in the Republican Party. Hopefully the 2016 presidential election will have the best winner.

NEXT 2 BLOW

Queen Breyon

Q. How long you been rapping and how would you define yourself as an artist?

A. I have been rapping since I was 7 years old. I sometimes got a chance to join rap ciphers at The Original Hip Hop Shop at a very young age. That's when I fell in love with what they call Hip Hop. It has always been a natural talent of mine that I realized I can take seriously. I have been pursuing my rap career on a serious level for a little over a year now.

Q. In pursuing your rap career, what have you accomplished thus far?

A. So far I have been recognized as one of the best female emcees from Detroit. I have also won a distribution deal for my single "Bring it Down" at the Music Hall. My biggest accomplishment so far is the recognition and title given to me based off my talent. My city has really shown a lot of love for this young girl with a gift and a dream.

Q. How do you feel about the level of hip hop females are bringing to the industry? Is it really Hip Hop or just doing music?

A. I feel like Hip Hop has not died, but is on life support and I can bring it back to life and set a tone for female emcees… and that so far the females coming in this game use they body to promote and only talk about violence and sex. I feel like it's a lot of male emcees that also have that tendency, but at least we have Jay-Z, Nas, Kendrick, and J.Cole to look up to for real Hip Hop. We had Lauryn Hill who has proved that a female can just spit and that she is the truth without coming out talking about sex and promoting sex. Let's promote having a good time, our community, and ourselves. Sex is a beautiful thing that's a part of life, but people talk about it so much it begins to lose value.

Q. Do you feel like there is a drought when it comes to women in the music industry?

A. Yes of course there is a drought and its hard being a female in this industry especially a talented one. It's harder the more talent you have. Women are only to sell sex… me I sell bars, talent, and Hip Hop.

Photography by
Jay Skillz 313

Q. Describe yourself as an artist and how you want people to internalize your music.

A. As an artist I'd say I'm truly inspired by life. I make it a point to be honest with my art; not real, just honest. I want my lines clever and relatable. I want my subject matter based on real life situations or emotions. I want my pain, passion, pleasure, ideas, and fears to be heard and voiced unapologetic. I don't have a genre; I'm a person so my mood and beliefs may change as I grow, as my understanding as a man grows, and I'm not afraid to show that.

Q. What personal experiences do you have that contribute to your music?

A. I talk about everything; about when my closest friends got locked up then emotions I dealt with dealing with them, they family, the block, and when they came home the growing part. I talk about my father who was a dealer and an user same time over in Zone 8. Growing up with that household missing regular kid problems working since I was 13 paying bills as a janitor through high school and keeping 2 jobs paying on my mom's bills and going to school.

Q. Describe what you've been grinding on in the studio lately and how you feel about your latest projects underway?

A. Currently I'm working on my newest mixtape entitled #hashtagabuse." It's just about finished we're just sprinkling it with cool. It's gonna be dope we have Freeway on a record, Ro Spit did a feature, Microphone Phelps, King Coda, and Nino Rossie who also did some production. I'm also working on a collaborative project entitled "Pixels" with Black Rain.

Q. SDM has interviewed Black Rain in the past and you have close ties with him so how did y'all meet?

A. I met Black Rain last summer at the jacking for beats competition Downtown Detroit. We both made it to the round before the final round where they picked the top five. He would've been number 6 and I would've been number 7 or around there. We clicked together

Monte SS

personality wise and been a unit every since.

Q. You indicated you got a song with Freeway so how did you manage to link up with him?

A. My former manager Schoolboy and I had a great idea for a big name artist feature so we started reaching out. Freeway happened to be in Detroit for a show with Jigga, and was doing an after party at Club Jaguar. Schoolboy chopped it up with his manager and thought it'd be a good idea to meet him before we record. That night we went and hung out with Free and his people, then Saturday morning he came to my crib and we recorded. It was dope because I got to see his process and how he creates.

Q. Describe yourself as an artist and what sparks your artistry?
A. I'm a true and passionate artist. I love all music! I love to perform! It's my way of expressing myself; it's an outlet and my therapy.

Q. What is a day like in your life and when do you find time to sing?
A. My everyday life is singing. A regular day for me is a studio session or teaching vocals (I'm a vocal instructor) and then rehearsals for shows or upcoming stage plays I'm in. Weekends are performances and gigs. God has allowed me and blessed me to be able to share, benefit, and live from my gift! It's my job and my career!

Q. What was the last showcase, last play, and last song you've performed?
A. The current play I am the lead role in is called Makin' Changes by Prince E. Mayes Sullivan. The last concert I performed at was Neo SoulSations with Avery Sunshine at Andiamos Showroom and my current single out

is titled "Don't Lie to Me" which I performed.

Q. Are you single, do you have children, do you have good management or are you chasing your dreams alone?
A. I have a loving boyfriend of four years and no children. I'm 19 so no! I have a great team behind me who supports every dream!

Q. Where do you see your music career in the next three years?
A. Well, I strive for it to be well in progress. I plan to have at least 2 albums released by then and on a world tour. I plan to be in many movies and even in a Broadway show.

Q. What is the biggest accomplishment you feel like you've made in your career?
A. The biggest accomplishment I've made is discovering who I am as an artist. I wouldn't even be able to call myself an artist without an original identity. A lot of people still don't know who they are as people so I consider me having an identity in my artistry as an accomplishment.

Johnyce

SNAP SHOTS

Email Your Snap Shots to
snapshots@sdmlive.com

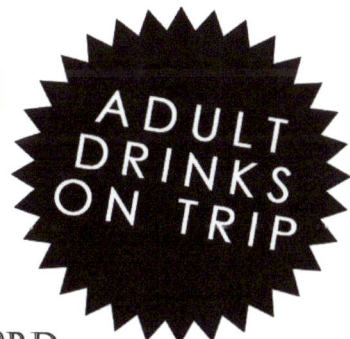

THE ALL NEW STYLE OF MAGAZINE-BOOKS

SDM